THE SOLOMON R. GUGGENHEIM MUSEUM

ISBN 0-89207-125-7 (hardcover)
ISBN 0-89207-126-5 (softcover)
Printed in Iceland by Oddi

Guggenheim Museum
Publications,
1071 Fifth Avenue,
New York, New York 10128

Designed by Cara Galowitz

Frontispiece: Fig. 1. *Frank Lloyd
Wright's signature tile, which he set
in all of his later buildings, as it
appears adjacent to the entrance of the
Solomon R. Guggenheim Museum.
Photograph by David Heald.*

Opposite page 1: Fig. 2. *Aerial
view of the Solomon R. Guggenheim
Museum, 1993. Photograph by David
Heald.*

CONTENTS

PREFACE

Thomas Krens

Although the Solomon R. Guggenheim Museum has occupied several different spaces in its fifty-seven-year history, for most people the institution is synonymous with its landmark Frank Lloyd Wright building. Since opening to the public in 1959, it has come to be recognized worldwide as an architectural masterpiece of the modern era.

Almost from the the time it opened its doors, however, the Guggenheim has posed myriad practical problems, ranging from lack of office and storage space to galleries that at times seem inhospitable to much large-scale art. Before Thomas Messer retired as director in 1988, he initiated plans for the construction of a tower based on Wright's original design for an eleven-story annex, which would act as a backdrop to the dominant sculptural form of the spiral museum. The addition, designed by Gwathmey Siegel and Associates Architects, was completed in 1992. It provides more administrative spaces, thus allowing public access to previously restricted portions of the original structure. Four new rectilinear galleries open onto the rotunda's spiral, providing an uninterrupted circulation pattern very much in the spirit of Wright's design.

Gwathmey Siegel and Associates also planned and supervised a major restoration of the Wright building. Guided by the desire to return all elements of the museum's architecture to their original state, the restoration process was as committed to historical accuracy as to preservation. The top-floor ramps, the skylighted bays, the small rotunda, and the original restaurant space are now completely integrated into the public presence of the Guggenheim Museum. The restoration of the Wright building and the tower addition have finally resolved a basic dilemma—the antagonism between the architecture and the art that it was meant to house—that has bedeviled the museum almost from its inception.

This book celebrates what is undoubtedly the greatest building of Frank Lloyd Wright's late career. In his highly informative essay, Bruce Brooks Pfeiffer, Vice President and Director of the Frank Lloyd Wright Archives in Scottsdale, Arizona, has shared his intimate knowledge of the sixteen-year-long process that led to the building's completion. His text is illustrated with many of Wright's astonishing renderings and plans. This book also benefits from a generous helping of photographs of this most photogenic building. Among them are photographs taken during the construction by William H. Short, Wright's Clerk of the Works, which are as remarkable for their documentary interest as for their artistic merit. David Heald, the Guggenheim's Manager of Photographic Services, has over the years created an extraordinarily rich body of images of the building, both bare and brimming with art. Photographs by Lee B. Ewing, former Assistant Photographer, make an important addition to this grouping. The beautiful presentation of these materials is due to the talents of Cara Galowitz, the Guggenheim's Manager of Design Services. This book was realized by our Publications Department, headed by Managing Editor Anthony Calnek. Production was managed by Elizabeth Levy, Production Editor, while many important editorial matters were handled with great skill and insight by Jennifer Knox, Editorial Assistant. Sincere thanks are also due to Pamela Myers, Administrator for Exhibitions and Programming, Stuart Gerstein, Director of Retail and Wholesale Operations, and Samar Qandil, Photography Coordinator.

A T E M P L E O F S P I R I T

THE COMMISSION AND DESIGN

Bruce Brooks Pfeiffer

On a summer's morning in Wisconsin, early in June 1943, Frank Lloyd Wright found among his morning mail a handwritten letter on small blue stationery, dated June 1 and signed "Hilla Rebay." The letter was a request—almost a plea—for Wright to design a new museum for Solomon R. Guggenheim's collection of non-objective paintings. In describing the works of art and the sort of building she envisioned for them, Baroness Rebay approached the affair with zealous enthusiasm, writing, "I feel that each of these great masterpieces should be organized into space and only you so it seems to me would test the possibilities to do so. . . . I need a fighter, a lover of space, an originator, a tester and a wise man. . . . I want a temple of spirit, a monument!" She ended the letter, "May this wish be blessed."[1]

"I appreciate your appreciation," Wright replied. "I would like to do something such as you suggest for your worthy foundation."[2]

Thus was initiated an intense era of work, of struggle—a saga—that would occupy Wright for the next sixteen years. No other commission in his long career consumed him as did this challenge to design and build the Solomon R. Guggenheim Museum. Toward the end of his life, when the building was under construction, Wright—who was noted for his fine health—admitted, "I have not been too well, as you probably have heard and part of my distress is due to the struggle over the Museum."[3] A month later, he wrote, "Since some fifteen years ago, I have fought steadily through thick and thin—through every sort of adverse circumstances and at great expense to myself to preserve the integrity of all this affair of building this new idea in museums according to the bequest."[4]

He endured the struggle, the adverse circumstances, and the fight simply to get a museum built unlike any other in the annals of architecture. When Wright and Guggenheim first met in 1943, long before any sketches or drawings existed for the project, Guggenheim made his objectives clear: "I do not wish to found another museum such as now exists in New York. . . . No such building as is now customary for museums could be appropriate for this one."[5] A contract was signed by Wright and Guggenheim on June 29, 1943, but it would be nine months before a definitive site for the museum was selected and purchased. During that time, ideas were coming to the architect, but without a specific site he believed he could not create a specific design. He expressed this anxiety to Rebay when he wrote, "I hope we can get a plot before [late January] as I am so full of ideas for our museum that I am likely to blow up or commit suicide unless I can let them out on paper."[6]

Within days of this letter, dated December 18, 1943, he had decided to start designing, site or no site. Wright's letter to Rebay of January 20, 1944, written while he was starting work on the Guggenheim design, puts on record a rare and detailed account of what was being, as he phrased it, "let out on paper":

I've been busy at the boards—putting down some of the thoughts concerning a museum that were in my mind while looking for a site. . . . If non-objective painting is to have any great future it must be related to environment in due proportion as it pretty much is already, not to the high ceiling. . . . A museum should have above all a clear atmosphere of light and sympathetic surface. Frames were always an expedient that segregated and masked the paintings off from environment to its own loss of relationship and proportion, etc., etc.

A museum should be one extended expansive well proportioned

Top: Fig. 4. *Taliesin, Frank Lloyd Wright's house in Spring Green, Wisconsin.*

Bottom: Fig. 5. *Taliesin, interior view.*

Page 4: Fig. 3. *Frank Lloyd Wright with George Cohen, the general contractor, during construction of the Solomon R. Guggenheim Museum, 1959. Photograph by William H. Short.*

floor space from bottom to top—a wheel chair going around and up and down, throughout. *No stops anywhere and such screened divisions of the space gloriously lit within from above as would deal appropriately with every group of paintings or individual paintings as you might want them classified.*

The atmosphere of the whole should be luminous from bright to dark—anywhere desired: a great calm and breadth pervading the whole place, etc. . . . Well, I've just had to get it out of my system and it is taking definite shape not as language but as a building adaptable to the New York plot. . . . When I've satisfied myself with the preliminary exploration I'll bring it down to New York before going West and we can have anguish and fun over it.

The whole thing will either throw you off your guard entirely or be just about what you have been dreaming about.[7]

Wright's allusion to a "well proportioned floor space from bottom to top—a wheel chair going around and up and down" gives the strong hint of a spiral plan. What was actually down on paper at that point has not survived. But what is clearly known about Wright's method of design he himself revealed to his apprentices of the Taliesin Fellowship when he said, some years later, "I never sit down to a drawing board—and this has been a lifelong practice of mine—until I have the whole thing in my mind. I may alter it substantially, I may throw it all away, I may find I'm up a blind alley; but unless I have the idea of the thing pretty well in shape, you won't see me at a drawing board with it."[8]

Wright's idea of using the spiral in a building predates his Guggenheim Museum design by nearly twenty years. In 1924, Wright designed for Gordon Strong a tourist facility on Sugar Loaf Mountain in Maryland in which three spiral ramps circumnavigated the exterior. Five years later, Wright wrote to Strong, asking him to return the drawings of the unbuilt project: "It seems something of the kind is contemplated on the other side, in France, only in that case, it is a *museum.* Some interest has arisen in this idea as I have worked it out for you and I have been asked many times to see it."[9] There is nothing before this rather enigmatic letter on record to give a clue as to the nature of the commission, and nothing follows. But it is quite clear that in 1929 Wright was considering the use of the spiral for an art museum.

Wright firmly believed that what he was designing for

Guggenheim would make the viewing and enjoyment of art a far richer and more meaningful experience than the traditional museum plan. In 1958, he wrote:

Walls slant gently outward forming a giant spiral for a well-defined purpose: a new unity between beholder, painting and architecture. As planned, in the easy downward drift of the viewer on the giant spiral, pictures are not to be seen bolt-upright as though painted on the wall behind them. Gently inclined, faced slightly upward to the viewer and to the light in accord with the upward sweep of the spiral, the paintings themselves are emphasized in themselves and are not hung "square" but gracefully yield to movement as set up by these slightly curving massive-walls. [10]

Early sketches reveal that Wright was not only considering the ramp for exhibition purposes and the sloped wall on which to place the paintings, but he was also concerned with the scale and the lighting of the interior. The ceilings were planned to be relatively low, in comparison with other museums, so that the public could view the art in a more intimate environment.

Placing the works of art in a setting of more human scale grew quite naturally out of his own experience with and preference about the display of art. At Taliesin (figs. 4–5), his home in Spring Green, Wisconsin, which he had begun in 1911, Wright displayed his own Asian art collection—Japanese folding screens, prints, and *kakemono* (hanging scrolls), Chinese landscape paintings, and wood, bronze, iron, and stone sculptures from both Japan and China—as an integrated feature of the interior. The screens were set flat against the walls and bordered merely by a strip of cypress to match the other cypress woodwork throughout the residence. *Kakemono* were similarly hung flat against the walls or stone piers. Japanese prints were matted in soft, tan paper and placed on specially designed freestanding easels. The wood sculptures were carefully placed on shelves and decks around the interior, while bronze, iron, and stone sculptures were placed outdoors in the gardens and courts. Everywhere, these works of art appeared in harmony with the architecture and extremely sympathetic to the overall environment.

Lighting played an important role in Wright's earliest drawings for the new museum. Besides the large dome over the central open court, another light source—a narrow, continuously running skylight—was planned over the sloped walls, in addition to fixtures for incandescent light installed in the same location. Wright explained to Rebay and Guggenheim that the inspiration for the direct lighting from wall and skylight also came from his own work space at Taliesin. [11]

With the ramp idea firmly fixed in his thinking (save for one flat-floor scheme), Wright proceeded to make several designs in order to study the one he finally wished to develop. Variations as to placement of the ramp and the color of material, for example, were carefully rendered as part of the initial set of preliminary drawings in 1944.

One of the earliest studies made by Wright (fig. 7) shows the elevation of the exhibition spaces with low ceilings in addition to several sectional drawings depicting the various ways of lighting the galleries to the left. This was followed by a hexagonal plan (fig. 9) for the gallery to the right and "the Monitor"—or office, staff, and residence space—to the left. The elevation (fig. 8) and view (fig. 6) that correspond to this plan show copper and glass tubes along with poured concrete. Immediately after he made this scheme, Wright changed the level floors to a sloping ramp, a concept that first appears as a "footnote" on the hexagonal plan, where he wrote "constant ramp." Wright drew another interior elevation (fig. 10) entitled "Various Allotments of Exhibition Space," denoting the ramp, and dated it September 1943. In the plan (fig. 11), a circular spiral ramp is placed to the right, the Monitor to the left. Each band of the ramp diminishes in size as it rises, permitting a continuous skylight to run along the outer, upper edge of the ramp (fig. 13). From this sketch elevation drawn by Wright, the study elevation (fig. 14) was developed by his apprentices. The final perspective (fig. 15) renders the building in rose marble. At the same time, Wright was considering a ramp that would expand as it rises, as the rather unusual sketch combining section and elevation shows (fig. 16). Here, Wright drew a cut-line down the central portion of the elevation so as to present a glimpse of the interior. To the right, he made a small "thumbnail" view of the museum. In the next four drawings he made (figs. 17–20), Wright developed the scheme shown in the sectional elevation sketch, with the ramp on the right-hand side of the site. Then Wright moved the ramp to the left side, as three

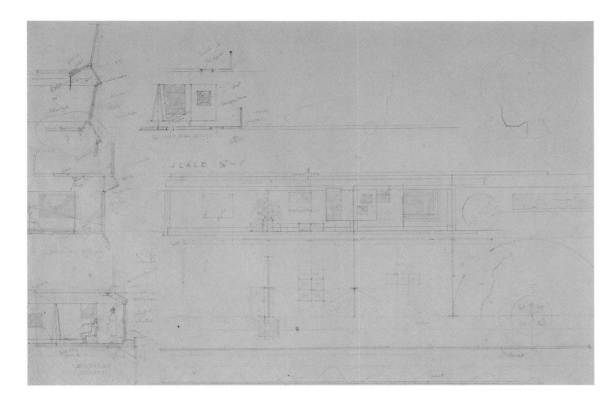

Far left: Fig. 6. *Perspective, 1943. Watercolor on paper, 50.8 x 61 cm (20 x 24 inches). The Frank Lloyd Wright Archives, The Frank Lloyd Wright Foundation 4305.748.*

Top: Fig. 7. *Sections (left), interior elevation (above right), and plan (below right), 1943. Pencil on tracing paper, 67 x 91.4 cm (26 3/8 x 36 inches). The Frank Lloyd Wright Archives, The Frank Lloyd Wright Foundation 4305.078.*

Bottom: Fig. 8. *Elevation, 1943. Colored pencil on paper, 50.8 x 62.2 cm (20 x 24 1/2 inches). The Frank Lloyd Wright Archives, The Frank Lloyd Wright Foundation 4305.006.*

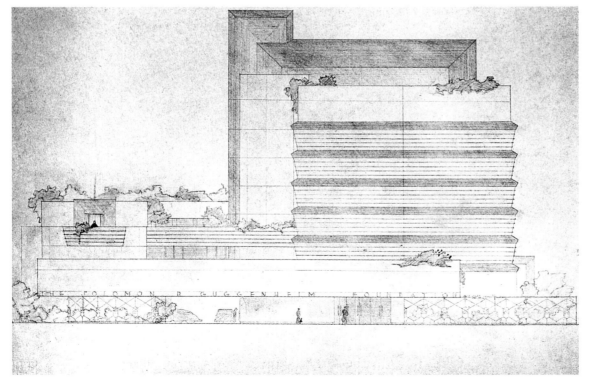

Top: Fig. 9. *Plan, 1943. Pencil on tracing paper, 47 x 93.7 cm (18 ½ x 36 ⅞ inches). The Frank Lloyd Wright Archives, The Frank Lloyd Wright Foundation 4305.091.*

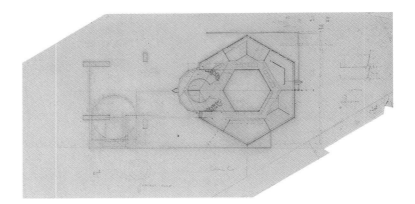

Center: Fig. 10. *Interior elevations and plans, September 1943. Pencil and colored pencil on paper, 50.8 x 61.6 cm (20 x 24 ¼ inches). The Frank Lloyd Wright Archives, The Frank Lloyd Wright Foundation 4305.002.*

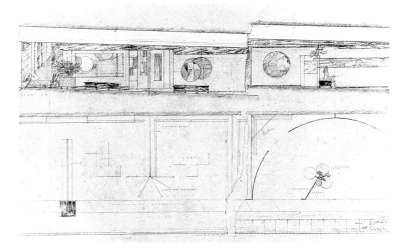

Bottom: Fig. 11. *Ground-floor plan, 1944. Pencil on tracing paper, 45.8 x 68.6 cm (18 x 27 inches). The Frank Lloyd Wright Archives, The Frank Lloyd Wright Foundation 4305.063.*

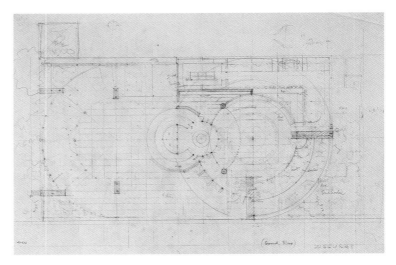

drawings—a sketch plan (fig. 21), a section (fig. 22), and a final perspective (fig. 23)—show. It was the final perspective drawing that Wright signed and placed on the cover of the group of sketches, which he then presented to Guggenheim and Rebay.

These early schemes were lavishly drawn up in watercolor, showing a choice of white, deep rose, or beige marble. The building was conceived as a poured-concrete structure, with the marble applied over it in thin sheets, like a membrane. The drawings themselves are unique in the collection: by this time in his career Wright was using graphite pencil and colored pencils for his renderings. (Occasionally, he would use a sepia or black ink, and sometimes he made what was called a "night rendering"—a drawing made on black illustration board with tempera and colored inks; see, for example, fig. 35.) But the set he made and then took to New York to show Guggenheim and Rebay was painted more than drawn, perhaps in keeping with the commission for a building to house paintings. "When [Guggenheim] saw the first sketches I made and that I took to him in New Hampshire at his request," Wright recollected, "he went over them several times without saying a word or looking up. Finally when he did look up there were tears in his eyes, 'Mr. Wright,' he said, 'I knew you would do it. This is it.'"[12]

Several plans and sections were incorporated into the set, and some elevations show the manner of hanging pictures. The interior elevations with paintings on the walls have a distinctively different feature about them—their frames, or more specifically, their lack of frames. In Wright's drawings, paintings are displayed with no more than a narrow, almost imperceptible band around them.

An interesting event happened in Wright's life at just about this time. His friend Georgia O'Keeffe had decided to give him her painting *Pelvis with Shadows and the Moon* (1943) some time before, but sent it to him only after her husband, Alfred Stieglitz, died.[13] Wright had seen it and other works at Stieglitz's New York art gallery, An American Place, and was especially taken by the method of framing. Wright noted this in his acknowledgment of the gift: "The masterpiece arrived properly framed! That is to say *none* showing."[14] The painting was framed in thin metal bands, one-eighth of an inch wide by two inches deep.

The site that was finally purchased for the museum, on the southeast corner of Fifth Avenue and 89th Street, turned

Fig. 12. *An existing townhouse at 1071 Fifth Avenue was home to the museum from 1947 until 1956, when the site was cleared for construction of the Frank Lloyd Wright building.*

Top: Fig. 13. *Schematic elevation, 1944. Pencil and colored pencil on tracing paper, 62.2 x 88.9 cm (24 ½ x 35 inches). The Frank Lloyd Wright Archives, The Frank Lloyd Wright Foundation 4305.076.*

Bottom: Fig. 14. *Study elevation, 1944. Colored pencil on paper, 50.8 x 61.9 cm (20 x 24 ⅜ inches). The Frank Lloyd Wright Archives, The Frank Lloyd Wright Foundation 4305.007.*

Far right: Fig. 15. *Perspective, 1944. Watercolor on paper, 50.8 x 61 cm (20 x 24 inches). Collection of Erving and Joyce Wolf. 4305.747.*

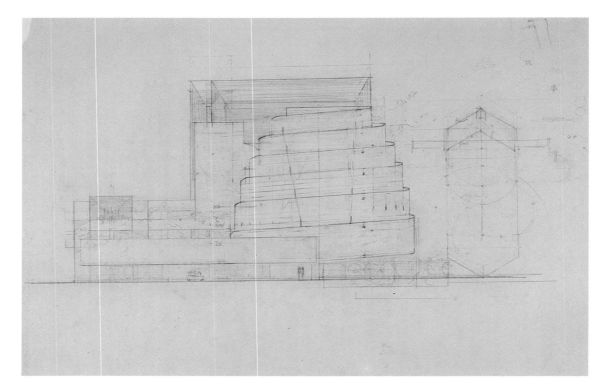

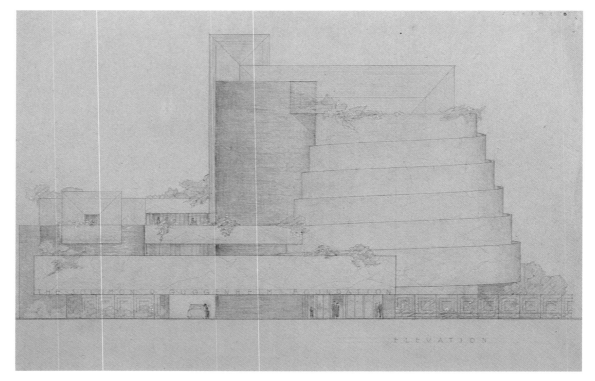

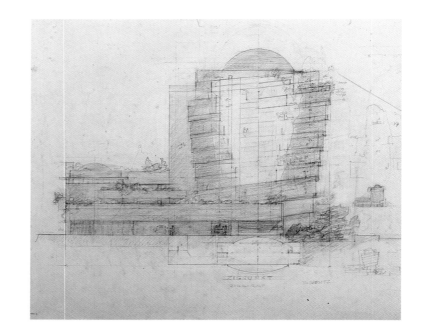

Top: Fig. 16. *Sectional elevation, 1943. Pencil and colored pencil on tracing paper, 66.7 x 77.2 cm (26 ¼ x 30 ⅜ inches). The Frank Lloyd Wright Archives, The Frank Lloyd Wright Foundation 4305.014.*

Bottom: Fig. 17. *Perspective, 1944. Watercolor and ink on paper, 50.8 x 61.6 cm (20 x 24 ¼ inches). The Frank Lloyd Wright Archives, The Frank Lloyd Wright Foundation 4305.746.*

Far right: Fig. 18. *Perspective, 1944. Watercolor and ink on paper, 51.1 x 61.3 cm (20 ⅛ x 24 ⅛ inches). The Frank Lloyd Wright Archives, The Frank Lloyd Wright Foundation 4305.745.*

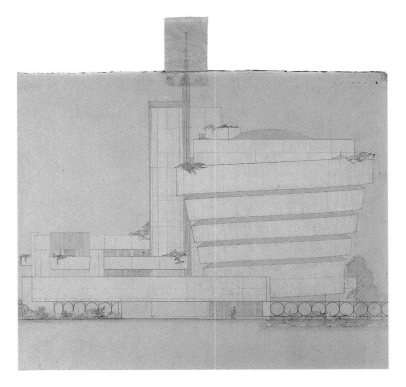

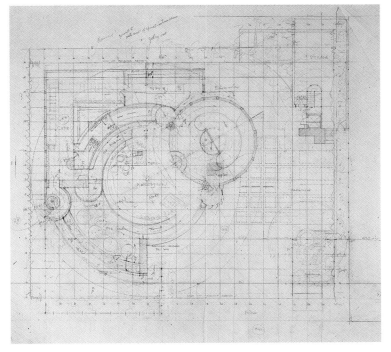

Far left: Fig. 19. *Perspective, 1944. Watercolor on paper, 50.8 x 61 cm (20 x 24 inches). Collection of Erving and Joyce Wolf.* 4305.749.

Top: Fig. 20. *Elevation, 1944. Pencil and colored pencil on paper, 60 x 61.6 cm (23 ⅝ x 24 ¼ inches). The Frank Lloyd Wright Archives, The Frank Lloyd Wright Foundation* 4305.025.

Bottom: Fig. 21. *Ground-floor plan, 1944. Pencil on tracing paper, 51.8 x 57.8 cm (20 ⅜ x 22 ¾ inches). The Frank Lloyd Wright Archives, The Frank Lloyd Wright Foundation* 4305.068.

Fig. 22. *Section, 1944. Pencil on tracing paper, 74.9 x 88.6 cm (29 ½ x 34 ⅞ inches). The Frank Lloyd Wright Archives, The Frank Lloyd Wright Foundation 4305.041.*

Far right: Fig. 23. *Perspective, 1944. Watercolor and ink on paper, 69.8 x 97.2 cm (27 ½ x 38 ¼ inches). The Frank Lloyd Wright Archives, The Frank Lloyd Wright Foundation 4305.008.*

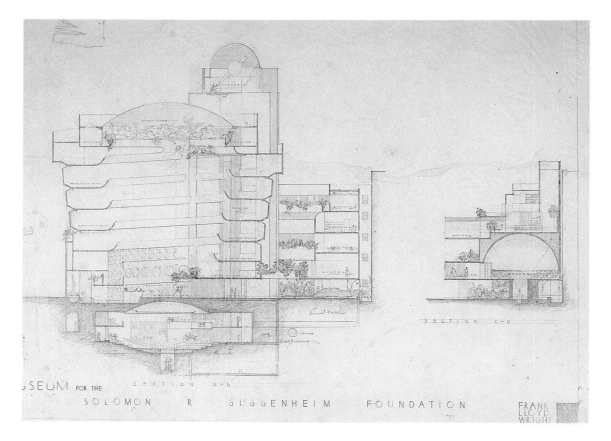

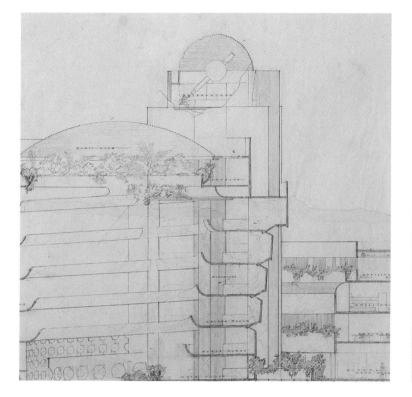

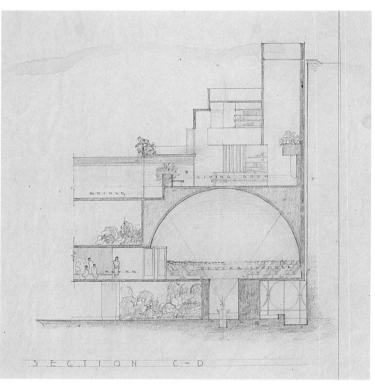

Above, left: Fig. 24. *Section (detail showing observatory), 1944. Pencil and colored pencil on tracing paper, 66 x 88.6 cm (26 x 34 ⅞ inches). The Frank Lloyd Wright Archives, The Frank Lloyd Wright Foundation 4305.035A.*

Above, right: Fig. 25. *Section (detail showing Ocular Chamber), 1944. Pencil and colored pencil on tracing paper, 66 x 88.6 cm (26 x 34 ⅞ inches). The Frank Lloyd Wright Archives, The Frank Lloyd Wright Foundation 4305.035C.*

Right: Fig. 26. *Section (detail showing auditorium), 1944. Pencil and colored pencil on tracing paper, 66 x 88.6 cm (26 x 34 ⅞ inches). The Frank Lloyd Wright Archives, The Frank Lloyd Wright Foundation 4305.035B.*

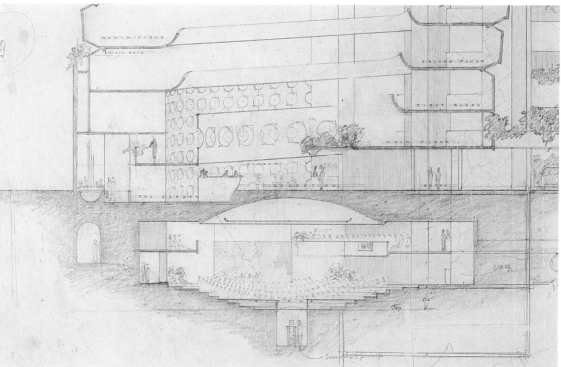

out to be only twenty-five feet less in breadth than the preliminary sketches had shown, which was "made up for by the additional depth," Wright wrote. "The area is nearly *almost exactly the same*—the Gods are kind."[15] Now the preparation of plans could go ahead in earnest. Guggenheim placed Rebay in charge of the project, and asked only that letters to Rebay be copied for him. During the ensuing months, Rebay's once-zealous enthusiasm gave way to doubts about the direction the new gallery was taking. In fact, the bulk of Wright's correspondence to her centered on trying to placate her fears and relieve her anxieties. It seemed that she still thought of a museum as a tall, square room. And to that end, a special "Grand Gallery" was designed (the present-day High Gallery) where larger, more imposing works could be exhibited. Wright describes his conception of the Grand Gallery:

The Holy of Holies should be on the main floor, not on the ground floor . . . The ground floor is never quiet. That will be impressively open above to the sky and on two sides to the park and be a general rendezvous—tea service from the kitchen, etc., etc.[16]

In July 1944, Guggenheim wrote to Wright assuring him that the preliminary sketches were entirely satisfactory and authorized him to go ahead with the next phase of the project, the production of the working drawings that would be used to construct the building. The first set—twenty-nine sheets of architectural drawings and thirteen of structural drawings—was signed by Wright on September 7, 1945. It reveals a structure quite different from what stands now. The character of the first set of drawings—seven other complete sets would eventually be made—is more in keeping with Rebay's initial idea of a temple to non-objective paintings.

In referring to the building and to public access within the museum, Wright often used the phrase "the downward drift." Clearly, it was his intention that visitors would enter the building, take the elevator to the top level, and begin their descent. From any place on the grand ramp visitors could see where they had been and where they were going. Wishing to bypass a section of the exhibition, they needed only to get back on the elevator and get off at the desired level. The Grand Gallery would be near the end of the tour,

and finally on the ground floor visitors would end at the front door, adjacent to a small café and tea garden.

Other aspects of the building, evident in the section drawings, reveal features not commonly associated with museum design. An observatory housed in a glass sphere was planned for the very top, off to the side of the rotunda (fig. 24), above the elevator machinery. In the auditorium beneath the ground floor of the main rotunda, seating was arranged so that the audience could recline, as in a planetarium, to view slides of paintings projected on the ceiling above (fig. 26). It was Rebay's desire that this viewing be accompanied by a string quartet playing Bach and Mozart! In the Monitor, adjacent but connected to the main exhibition ramp, was another, smaller theater, called the Ocular Chamber. Here the seats, as in the auditorium, reclined for viewing images cast up from a sunken central projector, but the surface for the images was a half dome (fig. 25). The Monitor held museum offices and apartments for Guggenheim and Rebay. Later, Guggenheim felt it prudent to remove living quarters from the museum. He reasoned that Rebay, in practicing her own work as a painter, would be free from curatorial distractions if she had an independent studio away from museum activities, while he himself already had a residence at the nearby Plaza Hotel. Consequently, a revision was called for; the section that had previously housed private apartments was turned over entirely to offices and staff workrooms. When Wright brought the drawings east and Guggenheim countersigned them with his initials, it seemed from that point on the building was ready to go into construction. World War II was over and building materials were now freed up from the war effort. But Guggenheim was of the firm belief that building costs, which were beginning to surge, would eventually go down. Thus, the construction of the museum was postponed.

Both Guggenheim and Rebay were convinced that a model of the museum was absolutely essential to explain the workings of its unique form both to themselves and others. Wright concurred with their wish and prepared a set of special drawings for the sake of making the model. By the end of August 1945, the model was completed and sent to New York. The first model (figs. 27–28) sent to New York in 1945 was made at Taliesin by Wright's apprentices, members of the Taliesin Fellowship. Constructed of Plexiglas, sections

Fig. 27. *Frank Lloyd Wright, Hilla Rebay, and Solomon R. Guggenheim with Wright's 1945 model of the museum.*

Top: Fig. 28. *Cross-section through Frank Lloyd Wright's 1945 model, showing the interior of the museum's rotunda.*

Bottom: Fig. 29. *Frank Lloyd Wright's 1947 model of the museum, view of Fifth Avenue façade.*

were heated so that they could be curved, then they were assembled and painted a cream color to represent the poured concrete of the final structure. Plexiglas scored with lines represented the glass tubing of the main dome, other glass areas, and the continuous skylight that wrapped around the exterior of the ramp. Glass tubes were first used by Wright in the skylights and partitions of the Johnson Wax administration building ten years earlier; he had found the crystalline light that emanated from the tubes most desirable. After being displayed in New York, the model was sent back to Taliesin, but it was irreparably damaged during shipment. In 1947, to reflect plans for an annex to the museum, another model had to be made (figs. 29–30).[17]

With the working drawings signed and approved by both architect and client, Guggenheim and Rebay once again began to express certain fears that the building would dominate the paintings and that the toplighted wall would provide inadequate lighting. Wright tried to assuage their fears in a letter to Guggenheim:

Now, to understand the situation as it exists in the scheme for the Guggenheim Memorial all you have to do is to imagine clean beautiful surface throughout the building all beautifully proportioned to human scale. These surfaces are all lighted from above with any degree of daylight (or artificial light from the same source) that the curator or the artist himself may happen to desire. The atmosphere of great harmonious simplicity wherein human proportions are maintained in relation to the picture is characteristic of your building.[18]

But the constant concerns, mainly on the part of Rebay, about the building dominating the paintings and about the lighting system continued to hound Wright year after year. He began to wonder, and asked in his letters to Rebay, why she had selected him as her architect in the first place. Although the model had been received enthusiastically, Wright increasingly began to doubt if Rebay really understood the building and its purpose. Guggenheim's faith in Wright, however, remained steadfast.

In 1946, two years after the initial property on Fifth Avenue was purchased, a narrow townhouse on the 88th Street side was also acquired, which the museum planned to use as its temporary quarters. Wright advised against investing large sums of money for a building that would eventually be torn down. He suggested, instead, that another structure, to be called the annex, be built to serve as a temporary gallery and office facility, but which eventually could be connected with the main structure. Guggenheim agreed to this, and Wright made the working drawings at great speed and sent them to New York.[19] At the same time, Wright made another perspective to show the addition of the annex at the rear of the museum (fig. 31). But again, Guggenheim, no doubt impaired by his failing health, procrastinated. Further revisions were made on the main building to try to lower construction costs, which were rapidly rising, especially in New York City. The architect finally promised Guggenheim that he would build his museum for the appropriated $2 million if he himself could make the necessary changes. Wright realized that Guggenheim's health was failing and wanted him to see the museum built. The architect revised the plans, proposing the removal of 380,000 cubic feet so that it would come closer to the appropriated sum. But Guggenheim refused to look at the plans when brought to him, saying, "No, Mr. Wright. I like it as it is. If we have prosperity what does a million more or less mean to me."[20] Filled with hope by Guggenheim's response, Wright wrote to Rebay in June 1949, "You say we might have started long ago. Tell me when. Meantime Life doesn't. The Cosmos sweeps onward and upward while we crawl on the surface like flies on a transparent window-pane."[21] Five months later, Guggenheim was dead. It seemed that hopes for building his memorial had died with him.

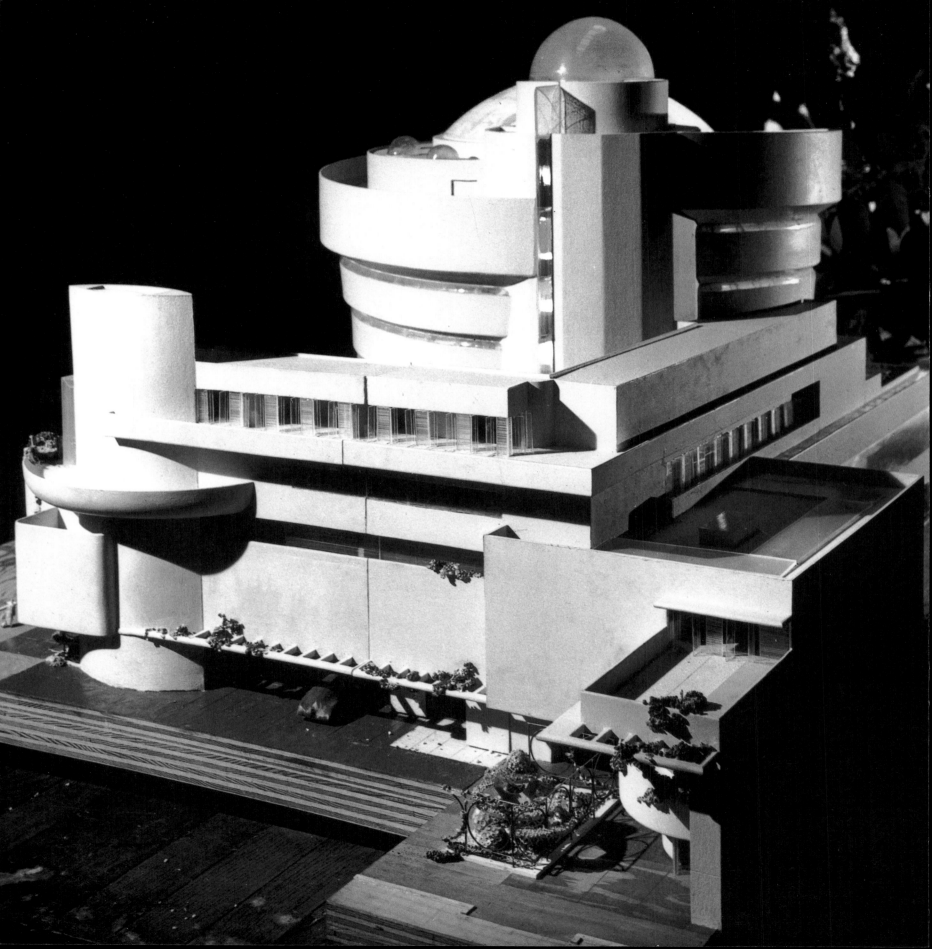

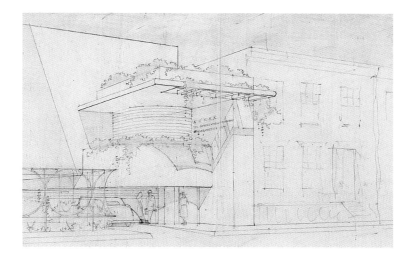

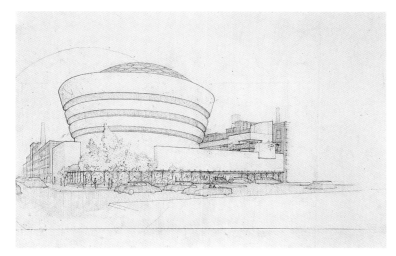

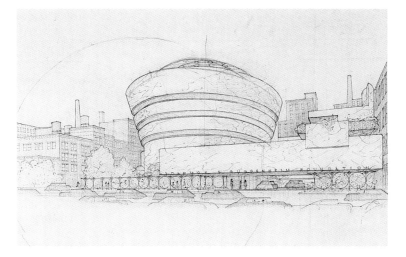

Far left: Fig. 30. *Wright's 1947 model of the museum, view of 88th Street entrance.*

Top: Fig. 31. *Perspective from 88th Street, 1947. Ink, pencil, and colored pencil on tracing paper, 50.2 x 73 cm (19 ¾ x 28 ¾ inches). The Frank Lloyd Wright Archives, The Frank Lloyd Wright Foundation 4727.013.*

Center: Fig. 32. *Perspective, 1948. Ink and pencil on tracing paper, 50.8 x 75.6 cm (20 x 29 ¾ inches). The Frank Lloyd Wright Archives, The Frank Lloyd Wright Foundation 4305.015.*

Bottom: Fig. 33. *Perspective, 1948. Pencil on tracing paper, 40.3 x 89.5 cm (15 ⅞ x 35 ¼ inches). The Frank Lloyd Wright Archives, The Frank Lloyd Wright Foundation 4305.016.*

THE MODERN GALLERY
MUSEUM FOR THE SOLOMON R GUGGENHEIM FOUNDATION
FRANK LLOYD WRIGHT ARCHITECT
HOLDEN AND McLAUGHLIN ASSOCIATES

Fig. 34. *Perspective, 1951. Ink,
pencil, and colored pencil on tracing
paper, 66 x 100.3 cm (26 x
39½ inches). The Frank Lloyd
Wright Archives, The Frank Lloyd
Wright Foundation 4305.017.*

In 1950, Harry S. Guggenheim, Solomon's nephew, was made president of the Solomon R. Guggenheim Foundation. Wright immediately wrote to him:

Never for a moment have I lost the feeling that here was the only American multimillionaire, who, when he died, instead of placing his means at the disposal of what passed for respectability in conventional art-museums—though laughed at by his friends—intended to face the future. He backed up his feelings as well as his faith by the liberal bequest to represent to the future a distinguished quality. *Other millionaires cuddled up to the Past for their memorial when they died. Not so Solomon R. Guggenheim. No. He died facing the way he had lived—forward.*[22]

Although he pressed for Harry Guggenheim's support in order to get the museum built, construction was again postponed.

In 1951, the remaining parcel of land was acquired. The full front on Fifth Avenue, from 88th to 89th streets, made a far more desirable building site than the one previously available. Wright went back to work to revise the plans accordingly. The large spiral ramp had been shifted from the south to the north side several times. Wright's earliest schemes, made before a site was purchased, show the large ramp to the right (equivalent to the south) side of the site. When the 89th Street corner parcel was bought in 1944, the ramp was relocated to the north, as in the drawings and in the models of 1945 and 1947. When the corner at 88th Street was acquired in 1951, the spiral ramp was shifted back to the south. For each of these changes, a new set of working drawings was required. After this last shift was made, Wright, in response to the changing administrative

requirements of the museum, suggested the construction of a tall building behind the museum for a historical gallery, staff offices, workrooms, and storage (figs. 34–35). Rising behind the museum would be an eleven-story structure containing private studio apartments that could be rented out as a supplementary source of revenue. It was this 1951 design by Wright that served as precedent for the 1992 addition of a "backdrop" building behind the museum.

In 1952, Rebay resigned as director. The museum was now moving in a new direction, expanding its collection, being rearranged along broader lines. With the appointment of James Johnson Sweeney to succeed Rebay, these programs demanded another set of changes in the architectural plans as well.

However tedious and time-consuming all these changes were, Wright was constantly improving the scheme to simplify the final result, which would come after another two sets of working drawings, in 1954 and 1956. All the while, the burden of making the building's cost commensurate with Guggenheim's bequest weighed heavily on Wright's ingenuity. Many details had to be sacrificed in order to stay within budget, but this was something at which Wright was a master. Over and over again he remarked that "limitations are an artist's best friend." No building in Wright's career illustrated this maxim better than the Guggenheim.

By 1952, the whole building had taken on a more unified, solemn appearance (fig. 36). Throughout the project's development, Wright was troubled by the vertical, unrestful nature of the spiral, although he knew it was essential to the purpose and design of the building. The first sketches show a horizontal form engaging the spiral and tying it to the Monitor; but by 1951 the horizontal band reaches across the

Previous two pages: Fig. 35. *Perspective, 1953. Tempera on board, 68.6 x 101.6 cm (27 x 40 inches). The Frank Lloyd Wright Archives, The Frank Lloyd Wright Foundation 4305.062.*

Top: Fig. 36. *Perspective, 1952. Ink on mylar, 77.8 x 110.5 cm (30 ⅝ x 43 ½ inches). The Frank Lloyd Wright Archives, The Frank Lloyd Wright Foundation 4305.306.*

Bottom: Fig. 37. *Perspective, 1957. Pencil on tracing paper, 83.8 x 127 cm (33 x 50 inches). The Frank Lloyd Wright Archives, The Frank Lloyd Wright Foundation 4305.009.*

entire Fifth Avenue elevation, both spiral and Monitor rising out of it. Yet again, in 1957, he further accentuated this horizontal band by having it protrude out, just before it reached 88th Street, and then continue back to engage the mass that houses the Grand Gallery (fig. 37). The space created by this extension was called the "Architecture Archive."[23] (In 1978, architect Richard Meier created the Aye Simon Reading Room in this space, connecting it to the main gallery via a keyhole-shaped doorway.) All of these design factors, intended to economize, strengthened the integrity of the design.

There was a brief span of time before the Guggenheim Museum was built when another Frank Lloyd Wright building stood on Fifth Avenue between 88th and 89th streets. This was a temporary pavilion that was designed to house a world-touring exhibition of Wright's work entitled *Sixty Years of Living Architecture* (figs. 38–39). The exhibition, which opened in January of 1951 in Philadelphia and was sponsored by Gimbel's department store, consisted of original drawings, architectural models, mural-sized photographs of executed buildings, and furniture and decorative objects. In 1953, it was installed in a pavilion that Wright designed for the exhibition on Fifth Avenue. Adjacent to the pavilion was a model home—a Usonian house—also designed by Wright specifically for the exhibition. Entrance for the public was through the old townhouse at 1071 Fifth Avenue, which was serving at that time as a temporary gallery for the Guggenheim collection pending construction of the museum. An archway in the north wall on the ground level led into the pavilion, which was roofed in glass and Masonite panels supported by a framework of pipe columns. When the exhibition ended, the pavilion was demolished.

As construction of the museum became imminent, consultations were necessary with Sweeney, Harry Guggenheim, and city officials over the building permit and construction details. For these sorts of discussions, Wright was usually able to assign his apprentices to represent him. His son-in-law William Wesley Peters was well trained, as both an engineer and architect, to handle the more complex jobs such as the Johnson Wax building. Other apprentices at Taliesin could manage the homes being built around the country. But the Solomon R. Guggenheim Museum was a job that Wright felt needed his constant personal supervision. In order to facilitate this, he decided to establish a New York office.

Although Wright was a great exponent of decentralization and a firm believer that cities were, essentially, evil, he could not conceal his love for New York. His favorite place to stay when in town was at the Plaza Hotel, which became the logical choice for an office. A two-room apartment with vestibule, kitchen, and bath was rented and refurbished according to his design (fig. 40). A sitting room served partly as reception area and office, while a bedroom could be screened off during the daytime and used for another office/drafting room. Sleek, black lacquer tables, easels, and hassocks were made by Wright's apprentices at Taliesin; the fabrics and carpets were lush and elegant—deep-plum velvet draperies and golden-peach wool carpet. The walls were covered in rice paper with gold-leaf speckles. Into this environment he brought some of his favorite works of oriental art from Taliesin along with the O'Keeffe painting, arranging them on easels along with a complete set of Sweet's Catalog File (a set of reference books for architects). After Wright's death in 1959, among his papers was found a "press notice" he himself had penned on Plaza notepaper just after moving into his new apartment/office. It reads:

Frank Lloyd Wright at the Plaza

He has always worked where he ate and slept and is doing so now with the air of magnificence and expense one associates with the Plaza. He has done the rooms over in the vein of the original Plaza as conceived by Henry Hardenberg {sic}—and managed at the same time to get a practicable working office, showroom, and sleeping quarters out of it—all pretty harmonious with Plaza elegance—with certain additions that Mr. Wright thinks would have pleased Henry Hardenberg {sic}. Unfortunately the apartment as it existed before he began it was not photographed so what happened is anyone's guess.

FLLW.[24]

On August 14, 1956, ground was broken. The construction contract was given to George Cohen of Euclid Construction Company. Wright appointed architect William Short as the Clerk of the Works. Short was to remain on site each day of construction, make certain that the architect's plans were

34

Top: Fig. 38. *Pavilion designed by Frank Lloyd Wright for the exhibition* Sixty Years of Living Architecture, *1953. View from Fifth Avenue. Photograph by Pedro E. Guerrero.*

Bottom: Fig. 39. *Interior view of pavilion for* Sixty Years of Living Architecture, *1953. Photograph by Pedro E. Guerrero.*

carefully carried out, and report to him on a weekly basis; he also documented the construction in a detailed series of photographs (for example, figs. 42–53). It must have seemed to Wright, standing in the excavated area where the grand ramp was soon to rise, that something of a miracle had taken place: thirteen years had passed almost to the month since the commission was given. Everything and everyone seemed to have tried to thwart its execution. Doubts and problems beset Wright at all stages. But now, during the summer of 1956, the building was finally rising, and continued to do so throughout 1957 and 1958.

A group of artists sent a letter to Sweeney and the trustees voicing their concern that any space with sloped walls and a ramped floor would be totally unsuitable for the exhibition of paintings. When confronted with this letter, Wright responded to Harry Guggenheim, assuring him that the design of the building would better serve paintings precisely because of the slanted wall, the skylight above, and the ramp for easy circulation. At the same time, Wright realized that Sweeney had very strong, and very conventional, ideas about the exhibition of paintings. One thing that Sweeney definitely did not want was to place the pictures on the sloped wall, as had been intended from the very start of the project in 1943.

To demonstrate to the trustees and director the manner in which the art could be best exhibited, Wright prepared a group of interior perspectives in 1958. On each drawing, he titled the placement of the exhibition area in relation to its "station" on the ramp and also gave the approximate sizes for pictures. Beginning at the top ramp was "The Watercolor Society," depicting paintings both on the sloped wall and on freestanding easels. Next came the "Average," meaning the general way of showing the oil paintings and freestanding sculpture, followed by the "Middle of the Road," halfway down the ramp, and finally "The Masterpiece," a large Kandinsky-like painting occupying one entire bay. The four interior perspectives made by Wright and his apprentices in 1958 also show his concern for the placement of hassocks and benches along the way. Sweeney chose not to follow these suggestions, and when the museum opened in October 1959 the paintings were mounted on pikes projecting from the wall, as if floating in a white void. Sweeney had insisted on an all-white interior, despite Wright's specification of a soft, off-white or cream color. The effect of seeing the vibrantly colored paintings, so unrelated to the architectural space and clashing with an unsympathetic dead white, was startling and disturbing. Right up until his death, Wright was involved in a bitter controversy with Sweeney over these matters.

When construction of the ramp had reached its top level by 1958, and the formwork had been stripped from the general ramp levels below, the public at large was able to get a glimpse of how the final opus would eventually appear upon completion. The building's exterior, nearly finished, caused even more of a furor than during the design phase. Artists continued to criticize the building as impractical for exhibition purposes, and the general public ridiculed its place on elegant Fifth Avenue. But the building was forged through to completion and opened to the public on October 21, 1959. By that time, Wright had been dead six months.

Two months before, Wright acknowledged the support of Harry Guggenheim when he wrote,

Dear Harry:

. . . I cannot tell you how much your reassurance means in this late day of the supreme effort involved in the museum. That you are prepared to stand by the philosophy that gave the building its present form. It is there in good shape and working against the odds you yourself have stood against and are experiencing—the transition from the carpenter and his square to the more liberal and universal atmosphere of Nature.

Affection, Frank Lloyd Wright.[25]

35

Fig. 40. *Frank Lloyd Wright's suite at the Plaza Hotel, ca. 1956. Photograph by Pedro E. Guerrero.*

Following page: Fig. 41. *The Solomon R. Guggenheim Museum, with Gwathmey Siegel and Associates' tower addition, 1993. Photograph by David Heald.*

Museums across the world seem besieged with the problem of space requirements as their collections and office spaces expand and the demand for more exhibition areas steadily increases. Added to these needs are the growing requirements for conservation and climate control. The Guggenheim Museum is no exception. Its expansion in both collections and programs has necessitated a series of physical changes to the building.

In some cases, the original intentions of the architect were either never fully carried out or they were drastically altered. The café on the ground floor, for example, was never executed; the conservation and framing departments were relegated to that area instead. Justin K. Thannhauser gave the museum a portion of his collection of Impressionist and Post-Impressionist art in 1963 on permanent loan. Since this gift was not part of the changing collection, the museum decided to convert space on the second floor of the Monitor from the library to galleries. These alterations were designed by William Wesley Peters of Taliesin Associated Architects.[26] An arched opening was cut through from the main ramp to connect with this new exhibition space. A portion of the fourth floor in the Monitor was converted to gallery space in 1980 in order to house an installation drawn from the permanent collection.

When the first change took place in the Monitor in 1963, Peters designed the annex, located on 89th Street, to house the offices previously located in the Monitor. With the thought of further expansion in mind, the four-story annex was built, in 1968, on a foundation that could adequately support ten floors when needed. The requirement for a bookstore space and the relocation of a tearoom was satisfied by enclosing the original drive-through passage between the rotunda and the Monitor for those two functions. But the major change that has occurred in the last thirty-four years is without a doubt the tower on 89th Street (fig. 41), rising six stories higher than the four-story Peters annex. This new addition, designed by Gwathmey Siegel and Associates Architects and completed in 1992, provides four floors of exhibition space, three of which are each two stories high, and two additional floors of office space. The tower engages the Frank Lloyd Wright rotunda behind the triangular stair tower at the second, fourth, fifth, and seventh floors, but does so in such a way that the drama and completeness of the main ramp is not impaired or disturbed. The lighting continues the sentiment that Wright employed in the rotunda: a general ambient toplighting with concealed focus lighting. The exterior limestone face of the new building resembles the original tall "backdrop" building designed by Wright in 1951. The café on the ground floor has been put in place as originally planned. The second, third, and fourth levels of the Monitor (rechristened the Thannhauser Building in 1989) now open onto the main gallery, providing three full floors for showing the permanent collection.

The restoration that was undertaken simultaneous to the expansion was greatly needed. New mechanical systems were installed, the continuous skylight cleaned and put back into operation, and countless details, after a period of more than thirty years, finally put to rights. The building emerges now more in keeping with Frank Lloyd Wright's design than when it opened in 1959.

Wright wrote "Ziggurat," the Mesopotamian word meaning "to build high," on some of the early studies for the Guggenheim Museum. Since the ramp of his building expanded as it rose, he referred to it as the "optimistic ziggurat." Certainly there have been other buildings

THE CONSTRUCTION

Captions for the previous
fourteen pages:

*Construction site photographs by
William H. Short*

Fig. 42. *Stacked pipes at the
construction site, ca. 1956–58.*

Fig. 43. *Construction of the main
rotunda, ca. 1957. Reinforcing bars
for the rotunda floor are laid in
preparation for the concrete to be
poured.*

Fig. 44. *Reinforcing bars,
ca. 1957–58.*

Fig. 45. *Construction of the main
rotunda, ca. 1958. At the fifth turn
of the spiral ramp, formwork is put
in place for pouring the walls of the
ramp bays.*

Fig. 46. *Formwork and reinforcing
bars, ca. 1957–58.*

Fig. 47. *Construction of the main
rotunda, ca. 1958. With the ramp
completed, formwork is erected for
the structural members of the
skylight.*

Fig. 48. *Formwork, ca. 1957–58.*

Fig. 49. *Construction of the main
rotunda, ca. 1958–59. The structure
of the ramp and roof is completed
before all exterior walls are poured.*

Fig. 50. *Construction workers at the
museum, ca. 1959.*

Fig. 51. *Construction of the main
rotunda, ca. 1958–59. View across
the structural members of the
rotunda skylight toward Central
Park.*

Fig. 52. *Poured-concrete walls of the
museum, ca. 1959.*

Fig. 53. *The main rotunda, 1959.*

Fig. 54. *Crowds attending
the opening of the museum,
October 21, 1959. Photograph by
Robert E. Mates (?).*

THE RESTORATION AND EXPANSION

Captions for the previous
four pages:

Fig. 55. *Construction of the tower,*
May 17, 1990. Photograph by
David Heald.

Fig. 56. *Tarpaulin covering the*
main rotunda during restoration of
the skylight, June 1, 1991.
Photograph by Lee B. Ewing.

Fig. 57. *Restoration of the main*
rotunda roof, March 27, 1992.
Photograph by Lee B. Ewing.

Fig. 58. *Restoration of the ground*
floor, Thannhauser Building,
September 20, 1991. Formerly used
for administrative offices, the space
now houses the Museum Store.
Photograph by Lee B. Ewing.

Fig. 59. *Restoration of the fourth*
floor, Thannhauser Building,
October 31, 1991, converted from
offices into exhibition galleries.
Photograph by Lee B. Ewing.

Fig. 60. *Restoration of the*
Thannhauser Building skylight,
January 2, 1992. Photograph by
Lee B. Ewing.

Fig. 61. *Crowds attending the*
reopening of the museum, June 28,
1992. Photograph by Lee B. Ewing.

THE MUSEUM AS A WORK OF ART

Captions for the previous
twelve pages:

Photographs by David Heald

Fig. 62. *Main rotunda ramp and
skylight, 1994.*

Fig. 63. *Triangular staircase,
adjacent to the main rotunda, 1994.*

Fig. 64. *Fourth-floor Thannhauser
Building terrace, 1994.*

Fig. 65. *Rotunda ramp, 1992.*

Fig. 66. *Rotunda ramp, 1994.*

Fig. 67. *Exterior of the main
rotunda, 1994.*

Fig. 68. *Rotunda ramp, 1994.*

Fig. 69. *Thannhauser Building
skylight, 1992.*

THE MUSEUM AS A PLACE FOR ART

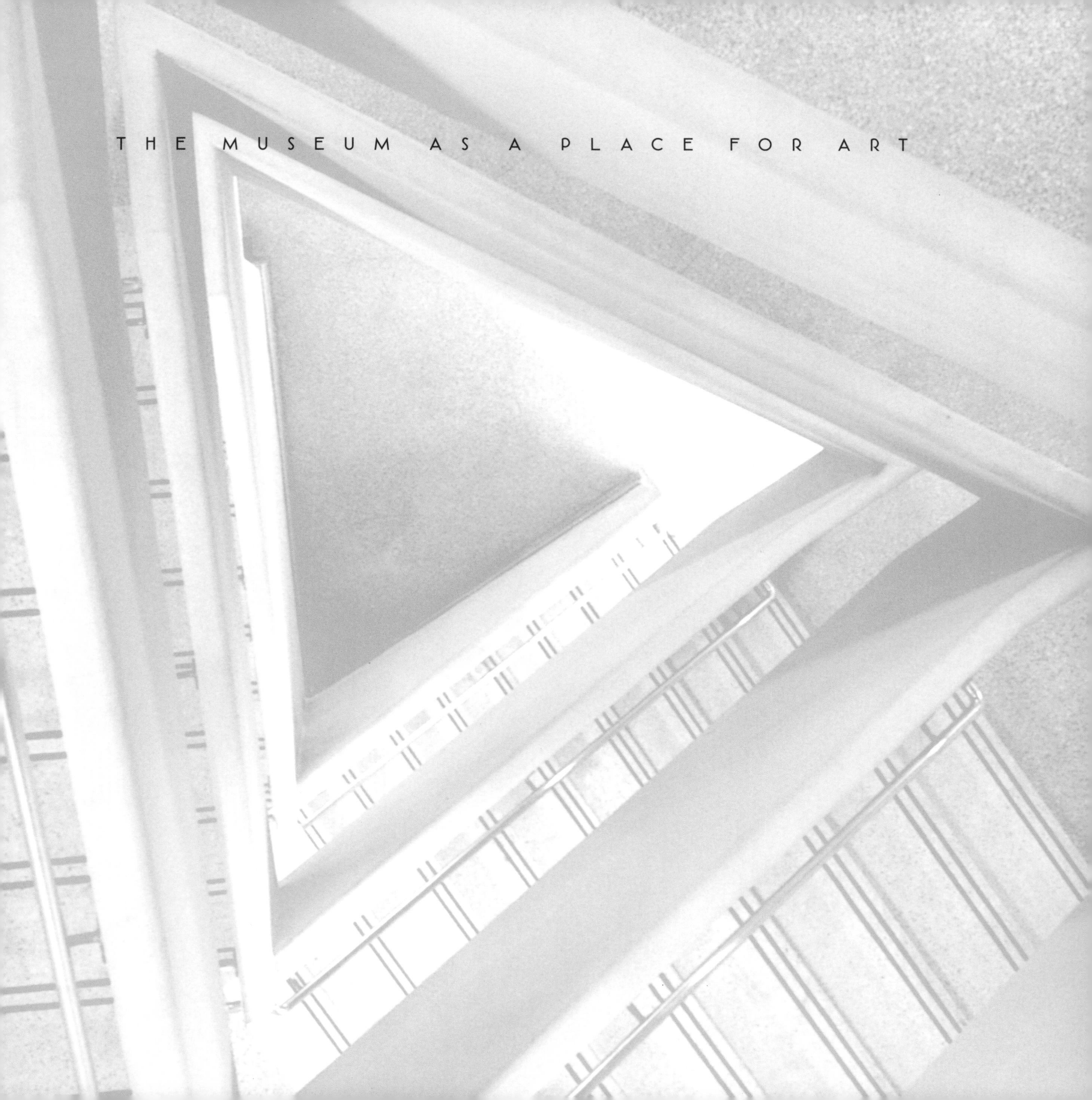

Captions for the previous
ten pages:

Fig. 70. *Architects and other guests
attending an evening in tribute to
Frank Lloyd Wright on the occasion
of the 125th anniversary of his birth
and the reopening of the museum,
June 24, 1992, with Dan Flavin's
site-specific work* Untitled
(to Tracy, to celebrate the love of a
lifetime) *installed in the main
rotunda and along the ramps as part
of the reopening exhibition*
The Guggenheim Museum
and the Art of this Century,
*June 22–August 27, 1992.
Photograph by David Heald.*

Fig. 71. *"Masterpieces from the
Permanent Collection" in the fourth-
floor Thannhauser gallery, installed
as part of the reopening exhibition*
The Guggenheim Museum
and the Art of this Century,
*June 22–September 7, 1992.
Photograph by David Heald.*

Fig. 72. The Great Utopia: The
Russian and Soviet Avant-Garde,
1915–1932 *in the fourth-floor Tower
Gallery, September 25, 1992–
January 3, 1993. Photograph by
David Heald.*

Fig. 73. America Invention,
*Lothar Baumgarten's site-specific
installation, in the main rotunda,
January 28–March 7, 1993.
Photograph by Lee B. Ewing.*

Fig. 74. *The exhibition* Picasso and
the Age of Iron *on the museum's
upper ramps, March 19–June 13,
1993. Photograph by David Heald.*